SCOTTISH PLACE NAMES

Nicola Wood

© Nicola Wood, 1989

Published by W & R Chambers Ltd Edinburgh, 1989
Reprinted 1989, 1990, 1991

British Library Cataloguing in Publication Data
Wood, Nicola
    Scottish place names.
    1. Scotland. Gazetteers
    I. Title
    914.11'003'21

    ISBN 0-550-20053-3

Cover design by John Marshall

Typeset by Bookworm Typesetting Ltd, Edinburgh
Printed in Singapore by
Singapore National Printers Ltd

Contents

Introduction

Many books have been written on the subject of Scottish place names, most of them longer and more scholarly than this one, which is presented as a kind of 'appetiser' for closer study of a truly fascinating subject. For those who wish to delve deeper, there is a bibliography provided. The book will perhaps also be of interest to those who are simply curious about some odd names they have come across. Since there is not room for anything like every Scottish place name in the body of the text, and so that readers may indulge in a little speculation of their own, there is a list of most of the common and some of the not-so-common elements to be found in the place names of Scotland.

It has been popularly supposed that Gaelic was the language spoken all over Scotland and that it was gradually supplanted by English. Although Gaelic was once spoken much more widely than it is today (its influence is presently confined to the extreme north-west mainland and the Western Isles), and the majority of Scotland's place names reflect this, this is certainly not the whole picture.

There are four major language influences, all of which have been adapted, corrupted and overlapped by the others to a certain extent. So we get names like Kinghorn, corrupted from the Gaelic *cinn gronn* (at the head of the marsh) and wrongly connected with the sad fate there of King Alexander III; Kyle of Lochalsh, romantically, and probably wrongly, interpreted as 'fairy straits'; and Methil, which combines words from Brittonic and Gaelic, languages whose influence and extent are outlined below. The field, therefore, can be a highly complex one and is still the subject of controversy, misunderstanding and 'creative thinking'.

Readers should not, however, be discouraged from making their own investigations and drawing their own conclusions, since, as might be expected, place names very often describe, in an obvious way, the land, its use, its features and its settlements.

Language Influences on Scottish Place Names

P-Celtic or Brittonic

This is thought to be the older of the two main Celtic language groups, its influence dating from about the fourth century, or even earlier. It was the language of the ancient Britons of Strathclyde (smaller than today's region of that name). The Picts, who probably inhabited the north and east of Scotland, remain elusive in every sense of the word, but recent research suggests that they may have used a dialect of Brittonic, although some claim a distinct Pictish language. For simplicity, the term Brittonic is used to cover both in this book.

Today, P-Celtic is represented by the Welsh, Cornish and Breton languages.

Q-Celtic or Gaelic

This second Gaelic language is now known as Gaelic and is spoken today in Scotland and Ireland, although in different forms. A form of Gaelic was also spoken on the Isle of Man, but this language is now almost extinct. The language was brought to Scotland from Ireland and gradually spread with settlers and Christian missionaries. By the ninth century, it had covered most of the Highlands and the north-eastern coastline and was beginning to encroach on the south-west.

Norse

Names of Norse derivation are to be found mainly in the Western Isles, Orkney and Shetland and the north and west coastlines, as these were the favoured landing-places of the Viking invaders and were where many of them ultimately settled. Historians agree that there were Vikings living in these areas by the early ninth century, but it has been suggested that the first settlements predate this.

English

English is, of course, the language of most of modern Scotland. It appears to have been well-established in the south-eastern and present border areas of Scotland by the 12th century and its influence on the place names there can easily be seen. Making steady progress thereafter, it finally reached the Highlands and Islands, where, however, Gaelic is still spoken as a first language in some areas. The Scots language developed from English.

Apart from the occasional Latin and French name (see Beauly and Linton, East and West), there is only one other influence of note on the place names of Scotland, but this is dimly comprehended as yet. Generations of etymologists have been defeated by certain, mainly water, names, which do not appear to fit into any of the language groups already mentioned, although tenuous links are claimed with some European water names. A pre-Celtic language has therefore been postulated, but as no significant body of evidence exists to support the theory, it remains a tantalising hypothesis.

Transplants

For every Scot living in his homeland, there appear to be at least two living elsewhere. The following list of overseas 'transplants' is testimony to their pioneering instincts.

Aberdeen Grampian
California, Idaho, Maryland, Mississippi,
N. Carolina, S. Dakota, Washington (USA); Hong
Kong; New South Wales, NW Territory (Australia); S.
Africa; Saskatchewan (Canada)
Aberfoyle Central
Queensland (Australia)
Abernethy Tayside
Saskatchewan (Canada)
Ailsa Craig Strathclyde
Ontario (Canada)
Alford Grampian
Florida (USA)
Alva Central
Florida, Kentucky, Oklahoma, Wyoming (USA)
Ardbeg Strathclyde
Ontario (Canada)
Ardrossan Strathclyde
S. Australia
Armadale Highland
W. Australia
Arran Strathclyde
Saskatchewan (Canada)
Ayr Strathclyde
N. Dakota, Nebraska (USA); Queensland (Australia)
Banff Grampian
Alberta (Canada)
Bannockburn Central
Ontario (Canada)
Bathgate Lothian
N. Dakota (USA)
Biggar Strathclyde
Saskatchewan (Canada)

Braemar Grampian
S. Australia
Brechin Tayside
Ontario (Canada)
Callander Central
Ontario (Canada)
Cardross Strathclyde
Saskatchewan (Canada)
Colonsay Strathclyde
Saskatchewan (Canada)
Cupar Fife
Saskatchewan (Canada)
Currie Lothian
Minnesota, N. Carolina, Nevada (USA); Tasmania
(Australia)
Denny Central
California (USA)
Dingwall Highland
Nova Scotia (Canada)
Douglas Strathclyde
Alaska, Arizona, Georgia, Michigan, N. Dakota,
Nebraska, Washington, Wyoming (USA); Manitoba,
Ontario (Canada); S. Africa
Dunbar Lothian
Oklahoma, Utah, Wisconsin, W. Virginia (USA);
Queensland (Australia)
Dunblane Central
Saskatchewan (Canada)
Dundee Tayside
Illinois, Michigan, New York, Texas (USA); S. Africa
Dunkeld Tayside
Queensland, Victoria (Australia)
Edinburgh Lothian
Illinois, Indiana, Mississippi, N. Dakota, Texas,
Virginia (USA)
Elgin Grampian
Arizona, Illinois, Iowa, N. Dakota, Nebraska,
Nevada, Oklahoma, Oregon, Texas, Utah (USA);
Manitoba, New Brunswick (Canada)
Elie Fife
Manitoba (Canada)
Fife Fife
Texas (USA)
Gifford Lothian

Florida, Iowa, Washington (USA)
Glamis Tayside
Saskatchewan (Canada)
Glasgow Strathclyde
Kentucky, Missouri, Montana, Virginia (USA);
Jamaica
Heriot Lothian
New Zealand
Inverness Highland
Nova Scotia, Quebec (Canada); Florida, Montana
(USA)
Irvine Strathclyde
Alberta (Canada); Kentucky (USA)
Islay Strathclyde
Alberta (Canada)
Jedburgh Borders
Saskatchewan (Canada)
Kelso Borders
California, N. Dakota, Washington (USA); New
Zealand; Saskatchewan (Canada)
Kilmarnock Strathclyde
Virginia (USA)
Kincardine Fife
Ontario (Canada)
Kinghorn Fife
Ontario (Canada)
Kirriemuir Tayside
Alberta (Canada)
Lanark Strathclyde
Florida, Illinois (USA); Ontario (Canada)
Leslie Fife
Arkansas, Georgia, Idaho, Michigan (USA)
Markinch Fife
Saskatchewan (Canada)
Melrose Borders
Idaho, Minnesota, Montana, New Mexico, Oregon,
Wisconsin (USA); Nova Scotia (Canada); W. Australia
Moffat Dumfries & Galloway
Colorado (USA)
Montrose Tayside
Arkansas, Colorado, Illinois, Iowa, Nebraska,
Pennsylvania, S. Dakota, Virginia (USA)
Nairn Highland
Ontario (Canada)

dun, dum	Gaelic *(dun)*	hill, fortress, mound
eccles	Gaelic *(eaglais)*	church
eder	Gaelic *(eadar)*	between
edin	Gaelic *(aodann)*	slope
elan	Gaelic *(eilean)*	island
ey, ay, a	Norse *(ey)*	island
fassie, foss	Gaelic *(fas)*	island
fell	Norse *(fjall)*	level place
fern	Gaelic *(fearna)*	hill
fetter	Gaelic *(fothair)*	alder
fin	Gaelic *(fionn)*	slope, gradient, hill
four	Gaelic *(por)*	white, bright
*gart, garth,	Norse *(gardr)*	pasture
gar	Brittonic *(garth)*	garden, yard,
	Gaelic *(garradh)*	enclosure
garve	Gaelic *(garbh)*	rough (water)
gil	Norse *(gil)*	ravine
gio, geo	Norse *(gja)*	chasm
glack	Gaelic *(glac)*	hollow
glen	Gaelic *(gleann)*	glen, valley
goul	Gaelic *(gobhal)*	fork
gower, gour	Gaelic *(gobhar)*	goat
ham	Old Eng. *(ham)*	village, farm, hamlet
howe	Norse *(haugr)*	mound
holm	Norse *(holmr)*	islet
ibert	Gaelic *(iobairt)*	offering
inch, innis	Gaelic *(innis)*	island
inver	Gaelic *(inbhir)*	confluence, mouth
keppoch	Gaelic *(ceapach)*	plot for ploughing
kil	Gaelic *(ceall)*	cell, church
kin	Gaelic *(ceann)*	head
*kirk	Old Eng. *(kirke)*	church
	Norse *(kirkja)*	
knap	Gaelic *(cnap)*	hillock
knock	Gaelic *(cnoc)*	hill
kyle	Gaelic *(caol)*	strait, narrow, slender
lagg	Gaelic *(lag)*	hollow
lax	Norse *(lax)*	salmon
leck	Gaelic *(leac)*	slab, flat stone
ler	Norse *(leir)*	mud
letter	Gaelic *(letir)*	slope, hill-face
lia	Gaelic *(liath)*	blue, grey
*lin, lynn	Brittonic *(llyn)*	lake, pool
	Gaelic *(linn)*	
loch	Gaelic *(loch)*	lake
lund	Norse *(lundr)*	grove
maddy	Gaelic *(madadh)*	fox, dog
mel	Norse *(melr)*	sandbank

mire	Norse *(myrr)*	swamp, mire
more	Gaelic *(mor)*	big
moy	Gaelic *(magh)*	plain, field
muck	Gaelic *(muc)*	pig
*ness	Norse *(nes)* Old Eng. *(naes)*	headland, promontory, cape
ochter	Gaelic *(uachdar)*	upper part, high place
os	Norse *(os)*	river-mouth
pit	Brittonic *(pett)*	part, share
plock	Gaelic *(ploc)*	clod, promontory
pol, pool	Gaelic *(pol)*	pool, pit
quoy	Norse *(koi)*	fold, enclosure for beasts
ra	Gaelic *(rath)*	fort
rioch	Gaelic *(riabhach)*	greyish
*ros, ross	Brittonic *(ros)* Gaelic *(ros)*	promontory, wood
set	Norse *(setr)*	house
sgor	Gaelic *(sgorr)*	rocky place
sheen	Gaelic *(sian)*	storm
sker	Norse *(sker)*	rock
slack	Norse *(slakki)*	depression
sten, stain	Norse *(steinn)*	stone
strath	Gaelic *(srath)*	valley
strone	Gaelic *(sron)*	nose, point
tay, ty	Gaelic *(tigh)*	house
tober	Gaelic *(tobar)*	well
ton	Old Eng. *(tun)*	homestead, hamlet, farm
tor	Gaelic *(torr)*	hill
tra, trie	Brittonic *(tref)*	homestead, hamlet, settlement, village
tulloch, tilly, tully	Gaelic *(tulach)*	hillock
voe, wall, way, vagh	Norse *(vagr)*	bay, creek
vik, wick, vig, bhig	Norse *(vik)*	bay, creek
wick	Old Eng. *(wic)*	settlement, place, farm
wra	Norse *(vra)*	corner

* There must be doubt in these cases which is the correct
    derivation.

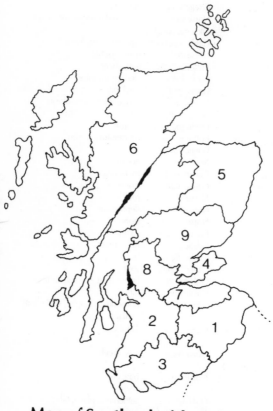

Map of Scotland with regions marked and named

SCOTTISH REGIONS

1. Borders
2. Strathclyde
3. Dumfries & Galloway
4. Fife

5. Grampian
6. Highland
7. Lothian
8. Central
9. Tayside

Bibliography

AA Road Atlas (Scotland), and *Illustrated Road-Book (Scotland)*.

The Place-Names of Aberdeenshire, William Alexander, 1952

Scotland's Place-Names, David Dorward, Blackwood, 1979

Gaelic-English Dictionary, Dwelly, Gairm Publications, 1901

The Place-Names of Argyll, H. Cameron Gillies, Nutt, 1906

Ordnance Gazetteer of Scotland, Groome, 1901

The Place-Names of Dumbartonshire, J. Irving, Bennett & Thomson, 1928

Place-Names (Introducing Scotland), Fiona Johnstone, Spurbooks, 1982

The Place-Names of Dumfriesshire, Sir Edward Johnson-Ferguson, Courier Press, 1935

The Place-Names of Fife and Kinross, W.J.N. Liddell, Wm Green & Sons, 1896

Macalpine's Gaelic Dictionary, MacAlpine & Mackenzie, Gairm Publications, 1971

Place-Names of the Highlands and Islands of Scotland, A. MacBain, Eneas Mackay, 1922

The Place-Names of West Lothian, Angus Macdonald, Oliver & Boyd, 1941

Scottish Place-Names, W.C. Mackenzie, Kegan Paul, 1931

The Place-Names of Galloway, Sir Herbert Maxwell, Jackson Wylie & Co., 1930

Place Names of Edinburgh and the Lothians, John Milne, McDougalls (facs. of 1912 edition)

Scottish Place-Names, W.F.H. Nicolaisen, Batsford, 1976

Place Names on Maps of Scotland and Wales,
Ordnance Survey, 1974
The History of Celtic Place Names of Scotland, W.
Watson, Blackwood, 1926
Selected Poetry, W.B. Yeats ed. Jeffares, Macmillan,
1962

I would also like to thank the many tourist authorities
of Scotland I rang up with queries, all of which were
answered with courtesy, speed and accuracy.

Scottish Place Names

A

Abbey St Bathan's   Borders

Baothen of Tiree was Columba's successor at Iona.
There was a 12th-century abbey church here. The Holy
Well of St Bathan's is in the grounds of the Manor
House.

Aberchirder   Grampian

'mouth of the dark stream'.

aber (Brittonic) mouth, confluence; *chiar* (Gaelic) dark; *dobhar*
(Gaelic) water, stream.

This is the smallest Royal Burgh in Scotland. It is known
as 'Fogie Loan' locally.

Abercorn   Lothian

'horned confluence'.

aber (Brittonic) mouth, confluence; *corniog* (Brittonic) horned.

Aberdeen   Grampian

'mouth of the River Don'.

aber (Brittonic) mouth, confluence.

The old town was built at the mouth of the Don and was
a Pictish settlement. There was another settlement, close
to the River Dee, on the site of what is now modern
Aberdeen. This has probably influenced the modern
spelling.

Aberdour   Fife

'mouth of the River Dour'.

aber (Brittonic) mouth, confluence; *dobhar* (Gaelic) water, stream.

Pronounced *aberdower*.

Aberfeldy   Tayside

'river-mouth of Paldoc'.

aber (Brittonic) mouth, confluence.

Paldoc was a follower of St Ninian and went to Fordoun, where a small portion of his chapel remains. Robert Burns wrote a poem called 'The Birks of Aberfeldy'.

Aberfoyle   Central

'pool-mouth' or 'the confluence of the stream'.

aber (Brittonic) mouth, confluence; *phuill* (Gaelic) pool.

The old village was 1 mile east of the present village and was written of in Sir Walter Scott's novel *Rob Roy*.

Aberlady   Lothian

probably 'bay' or 'port of the lady', 'lady' being the Virgin Mary.

aber (Brittonic) in this example, bay or port, estuary; *hlaefdig* (Old English) lady.

The ruins of the ancient Mary's Chapel are in the churchyard.

Aberlemno   Tayside

'mouth of the elm-stream'.

aber (Brittonic) mouth, confluence; *leamhan* (Gaelic) elm.

Abernethy   Tayside

'mouth of the Nethy'.

aber (Brittonic) mouth, confluence.

Maybe an early form of the Gaelic *an eitighich* which means 'at the narrow opening' (literally, gullet). This village was once a Pictish capital.

Abington   Strathclyde

'village of Albin'.

tun (Old English) farm, homestead, village.

Aboyne   Grampian

'ford of the white cows'.

ath (Gaelic) ford; *bo* (Gaelic) cows, cattle; *fionn* (Gaelic) white.

Aboyne Castle is home for the Gordon clan.

Achanalt   Highland

'field by the stream'.

achadh (Gaelic) field; *allt* (Gaelic) stream, burn.

Achiltibuie   Highland

probably 'field of the yellow rivulet'.

achadh (Gaelic) field; *uillt* (Gaelic) rivulet, brook; *buidhe* (Gaelic) yellow.

Pronounced *achiltybooey*. It is said locally that the true meaning is 'field of the yellow-haired lad' (*achadh a guille buidhe*).

Achnacarry   Highland

'field of the fish-trap'.

achadh (Gaelic) field; *caraidh* (Gaelic) fish-trap, weir.

Achnacarry House is the seat of Cameron of Lochiel, chief of the Clan Cameron. One of the clan's most famous chiefs was a supporter of Bonnie Prince Charlie at the time of the 1745 Rebellion. The house was used as a commando training centre during World War II.

Achnacloich   Highland

'field of the stone'.

achadh (Gaelic) field; *clach* (Gaelic) stone.

3

Achnasheen   Highland
'field of storms'.
achadh (Gaelic) field; *sian* (Gaelic) storm.

Achnashellach   Highland
'field of willows'.
achadh (Gaelic) field; *seilach* (Gaelic) willow.

Affleck   Grampian
'stony field'.
achadh (Gaelic) field; *leac* (Gaelic) flat stone.

Affric   Highland
possibly 'ford of the boar'.
ath (Gaelic) ford; *bhraich* (Gaelic) boar.
The name may derive from that of a Celtic water-nymph.
The BBC television series *Last of the Mohicans* was
filmed at Affric. It is not known if the tribe is still living in
the area.

Airdrie   Strathclyde
'high slope'.
ard (Gaelic) high; *ruighe* (Gaelic) slope.

Alexandria   Strathclyde
Named after Alexander Smollett, MP for Bonhill in 1760.
Tobias Smollett, the novelist, was born here in 1721.

Alford   Grampian
probably 'high ford'.
ath (Gaelic) ford; *aird* (Gaelic) high.
Pronounced *ahferd*.

Alloa   Central

'rocky place'.

ail (Gaelic) rock.

Alloway, Alva, Alyth and **Alves** probably owe their names to the same root.

Alness   Highland

probably 'holy river'.

This is a pre-Celtic river name.

Alves   Grampian

'rocky place'.

ail (Gaelic) rock.

Macbeth's meeting-place with the three witches is nearby.

Amisfield   Dumfries & Galloway

Amyas de Charteris was an early lord of the manor. The 16th-century Amisfield Tower is the seat of the Charteris family. Pronounced *aimsfield*.

Annan   Dumfries & Galloway

possibly 'swift river'.

an or *ant* are common endings to Celtic river names. Variations are found in Wales, Ireland, England and Brittany.

Anstruther   Fife

'the little stream'.

an (Gaelic) the; *sruthair* (Gaelic) little stream.

The town is divided by the harbour into Anstruther Easter and Anstruther Wester.

Appin   Strathclyde

'abbeylands'.

apuinn (Gaelic) abbeylands.

This probably refers to Moluag's community at Lismore. The area is featured in Robert Louis Stevenson's *Kidnapped*. In 1752, Colin Campbell, known as 'The Red Fox', was murdered here. His alleged killer was eventually hanged after what many considered was an unfair trial.

Applecross   Highland

'mouth of the River Crossan'.

aber (Brittonic) mouth, confluence; *crossain* (Gaelic) little cross.

A monastery was founded here in AD 673 by the Celtic saint Maelrubba. His name is also connected with Amulree, which means Maelrubba's ford. Popular myth has it that the name originated from the crab-apple trees, or, alternatively, the stone crosses which marked out an area within which one could take sanctuary.

Arbroath   Tayside

'mouth of the Brothock Water'.

aber (Brittonic) mouth, confluence; *brothach* (Gaelic) boiling, turbulent.

Arbroath is a shortened version of the town's old name Aberbrothock. Scotland's Declaration of Independence was signed here in 1320, by Robert the Bruce.

Ardchattan   Strathclyde

'point of St Catan'.

ard (Gaelic) point, cape, height.

Ardersier   Highland

'high west point'.

aird (Gaelic) high, height; *ros* (Gaelic) point; *iar* (Gaelic) west.

Ardgour   Highland

'Gabran's point'.

ard (Gaelic) point, cape, height; or possibly 'goat point': *gobhar* (Gaelic) goat.

Ardmore   Highland

'big cape'.

ard (Gaelic) cape, point, height; *mor* (Gaelic) big.

Ardnamurchan   Highland

probably 'point of the sea-otters'.

ard (Gaelic) cape, point, height; *muirchu* (Gaelic) sea-otter (sea-hound).

It may be, however, that the second part of this name is *muirchol*, meaning sea-wickedness, referring to piracy.

Ardrishaig   Strathclyde

'thorny height'.

ard (Gaelic) point, cape, height; *dris* (Gaelic) thorns, brambles.

Ardrossan   Strathclyde

'cape of the little cape'.

ard (Gaelic) cape, point, height; *rossan* (Gaelic) little cape.

As you might guess, Ardrossan is by the sea.

Arisaig   Highland

'bay of Aros'.

vik (Norse) bay.

Armadale   Highland

'dale of arms'.

dol (Brittonic) dale, valley.

Arrochar   Strathclyde

This name stems from the Latin *aratrum*, meaning a land measurement, called a ploughgate in Scots. The area was 104 acres of land. This was calculated on the basis that an ox could work 13 acres of land in a year (13 acres, therefore, were called an oxgate) and eight oxen attached to a plough could work a ploughgate.

Arran, Isle of   Strathclyde

'high place'.

aran (Brittonic) high place.

The highest point in Arran is called Goat Fell (or Cow Slip, as one enlightened child described it).

Athelstaneford   Lothian

This was the scene of the defeat of Athelstan, a Northumbrian leader, in the eighth century.

Auchencairn   Dumfries & Galloway

'field of the cairn'.

achadh (Gaelic) field.

A cairn is a pile of stones, built to commemorate the dead, or some notable event. Here, it is a burial cairn.

Auchendinny   Lothian

probably 'field of fire'.

achadh (Gaelic) field; *teine* (Gaelic) fire.

Auchinleck   Strathclyde

'field of the flat stone'.

achadh (Gaelic) field; *leac* (Gaelic) flat stone.

James Boswell, the famous biographer of Dr Johnson, is buried here.

Auchterarder   Tayside

'upland of high water'.

uachdar (Gaelic) upland; ard (Gaelic) high, height; *dobhar* (Gaelic) water.

Auchtermuchty   Fife

'upland for swine'.

uachdar (Gaelic) upland; *muc* (Gaelic) swine.

Aviemore   Highland

'big hill-face'.

aghaidh (Gaelic) hill-face; *mor* (Gaelic) big.

The 'big hill-faces' here are much used for skiing.

Ayr   Strathclyde

an ancient water name.

The town stands on the River Ayr. John Macadam (as in tarmac) was born here in 1756.

B

Badenoch   Highland
'marshy land'.
baidheanach (Gaelic) drowned land.
So called because of flooding from the River Spey.

Balerno   Lothian
'sloe-tree farm'.
baile (Gaelic) village, homestead; *airneach* (Gaelic) sloe-tree.

Ballachulish   Highland
'village on the straits'.
baile (Gaelic) village, homestead; *caolas* (Gaelic) straits, narrows.
This area is described by Robert Louis Stevenson in his book *Kidnapped*.

Ballantrae   Strathclyde
'village on the shore'.
baile (Gaelic) village, homestead; *traigh* (Gaelic) beach, shore.
See Robert Louis Stevenson's book *The Master of Ballantrae*.

Ballater Grampian

'pass-land' or possibly 'broom-land'.

bealach (Gaelic) pass, road; *bealaidh* (Gaelic) broom; *tir* (Gaelic) land.

Balmoral Grampian

probably 'village in the big clearing'.

baile (Gaelic) village, homestead; *mor* (Gaelic) big; *ial* (Brittonic) clearing.

It has been suggested that the name could mean 'majestic' or 'splendid' village, from the Gaelic *morail*. The fact that Queen Victoria built a large house here and that it is the Queen's present summer residence lends itself to this interpretation, but it has been discounted.

Balquhidder Central

'woodland village'.

baile (Gaelic) village, homestead; *fid tir* (Gaelic) woodland.

Rob Roy Macgregor, hero of Sir Walter Scott's famous novel *Rob Roy*, is buried here.

Pronounced *balwhidder*.

Banchory Grampian

'high place'.

beannachar (Gaelic) high place.

Banff Grampian

possibly 'land unploughed for one year'.

banbh (Gaelic).

Connections have also been suggested, however, with *Banba*, a Gaelic word for Ireland. The remains of Macduff's castle stand here.

Bannockburn   Central

'bright water'.

bhan (Brittonic) bright; *oc, ach* (Brittonic) water.

Bannockburn is famous mainly for the great battle which took place in 1314, when Robert the Bruce and his men defeated the army of Edward II of England.

Barra, Isle of   Western Isles

'St Barr's island'.

Several carved slabs can still be seen at Cille-bharra, where once the church of St Barr stood.

Barlinnie   Strathclyde

'height with a pool'.

barr (Gaelic) height, top; *llyn* (Brittonic) pool, linn.

Barlinnie is famous (or infamous) for its prison, which was once the home of Jimmy Boyle, Glasgow villain turned sculptor and general raconteur.

Bathgate   Lothian

'house in the wood', or perhaps 'boar-wood'.

both (Brittonic) house, bothy; *cett* (Brittonic) wood; *baedd* (Brittonic) boar.

This is the birthplace in 1811 of Sir James Simpson, who championed the use of chloroform as an anaesthetic.

Beauly   Highland

'lovely place'.

beau lieu (French).

Bellahouston   Strathclyde

'village with the crucifix'.

baile (Gaelic) village, homestead; *cheusadain* (Gaelic) crucifix.

Benbecula, Isle of   Western Isles

perhaps 'herdsman's hill'.

beinn (Gaelic) hill; *buachaill* (Gaelic) herdsman.

This may have been one of many similar names, used to identify a hill on which a herdsman could stand and survey his 'territory'.

Berwick, North   Lothian

'barley farm'.

bere (Old English) barley; *wic* (Old English) settlement, farm.

Bettyhill   Highland

Named after Elizabeth, Countess of Sutherland, this small village was built c.1820 to provide housing for some of those who were homeless as a result of the Highland Clearances.

Biggar   Strathclyde

'barley field'.

bygg (Norse) barley; *gardr* (Norse) enclosed field of crops.

Birnam   Tayside

'village of the warrior'.

biorn (Old English) warrior; *ham* (Old English) home, village.

There are two trees here which are claimed to be the small remainder of Birnam Wood, immortalised by Shakespeare in *Macbeth*.

Bishopbriggs   Strathclyde

'bridge of the Bishop of Glasgow'.

Blair Atholl   Tayside

'the new Ireland'.

blar (Gaelic) plain, piece of cleared land; *ath Fhodla* (Gaelic) the next, or new, Ireland.

Blair Castle is the home of the Duke of Atholl and dates back to 1269. The Duke has the only private army, complete with fine pipe band, in Britain.

Blairgowrie   Tayside

'plain of Gowrie'.

blar (Gaelic) plain, piece of cleared land.

Gabran (Gowrie) was the son of Fergus, a legendary Irish leader.

Blantyre   Strathclyde

'end-land'.

blaentir (Brittonic) edge, end-land.

In 1813, the famous explorer David Livingstone was born here.

Boat of Garten   Highland

The name refers to the ferry that used to cross the River Garten before a bridge was built in 1898. The place has been well publicised as a nesting-place for ospreys.

Bonaly   Lothian

'house on the hill'.

both (Gaelic) house, hut; *na h'aile* (Gaelic) on the hill.

Bo'ness   Central

in full, Borrowstounness 'headland of the burgh town'.

borrowstoun (Scots) a royal burgh: *burh* (Old English) fortified town, village; *tun* (Old English) hamlet, homestead; *naes* (Old English) headland.

There is a pirates' graveyard here.

Braemar   Grampian

'upper part of Mar'.

braighe (Gaelic) upper part of the country.

Mar was a local family name. Braemar is famous for its Highland Games, which take place each summer and are attended by the Queen.

Breadalbane   Central

'the heights of Alba'.

braighe (Gaelic) upper slope, heights.

Albyn is an ancient name for Scotland.

Brechin   Tayside

'Brychan's place'.

Brychan was an Irish prince.

Bridge of Allan   Central

'bridge over Allan Water'.

Brodick   Isle of Arran, Strathclyde

'broad bay'.

breidr (Norse) broad; *vik* (Norse) bay.

Brora   Highland

'bridge river'.

bru (Norse) bridge; *a* (Norse) river.

Brora bridge was the only bridge in Sutherland before the 19th century.

Broxburn   Lothian

probably 'badger's stream'.

broc (Gaelic) badger; *burna* (Old English) stream; but maybe a tautologous word, *broc* (Old English) brook, stream.

Buccleuch   Borders

probably 'buck's gorge'.

buk (Old English) buck; *cloghe* (Middle English) glen, gorge.

Pronounced *bucklew*.

Burdiehouse   Lothian

Legend has it that this is 'Bordeaux house' and somehow associated with the retinue of Mary, Queen of Scots.

Burntisland   Fife

maybe 'Burnet's land'.

The origin of this name is obscure. There is a story which tells of a fire on a small island close to shore, but this is not confirmed.

Bute, Isle of   Western Isles

This is an old name for Rothesay, or Roderick's Island. It possibly derives from *bot*, Norse for a patch of land.

C

Caerlaverock   Dumfries & Galloway

'fortress in the elm-wood'.

cathair (Gaelic) fortress; *leamhreaich* (Gaelic) elm-wood.

Caerlaverock Castle is said to be the 'Ellengowan' in Sir Walter Scott's *Guy Mannering.*

Cairngorm   Highland

'greeny blue hill'.

carn (Gaelic) heap of stones, hill; *gorm* (Gaelic) green/blue.

The word 'cairn' is often used to mean a hill. Its other common meaning is a pile of stones built as a memorial of the dead.

Calder, East and West   Highland and Lothian

'rapid river' or 'hard, stony river'.

callaidh (Gaelic) rapid; *caladh* (Gaelic) hard, stony; *dobhar* (Gaelic) water, river.

Callander   Central

probably has the same root as Calder.

Callander was 'Tannochbrae' in the very successful BBC television series *Dr Finlay's Casebook'.*

Cambuslang   Strathclyde

'ship-bay' or 'ship-creek'.

camas (Gaelic) bay, creek, bend; *long* (Gaelic) ship.

The settlement used to be known as Cambuslong.

Campbeltown   Strathclyde

Formerly Kilkerran, 'head of St Ciaran's loch', the town was renamed after the Earl of Angus, head of Clan Campbell. Campbeltown Loch is fixed in the minds of Scots as the title of a song about a man who wishes the loch was full of whisky instead of water.

Cannich   Highland

'white river'.

can (Gaelic) white, fair, and possibly *och* (Brittonic) water.

Canonbie   Dumfries & Galloway

'canon's village'.

byr (Norse) farm, village.

The old Priory of Canonbie was destroyed in 1542.

Canisbay   Highland

probably has the same root as Canonbie.

Cardross   Strathclyde

'copse point'.

carden (Brittonic) copse, thicket; *ros* (Brittonic) point.

Formerly Cardinross, Robert the Bruce died here in 1329.

Carnoustie   Tayside

'rock of the pinewood'.

carraig (Gaelic) rock; *giuthas* (Gaelic) pine- or fir-wood.

The British Open Golf Tournament is played here from time to time.

Castle Douglas   Dumfries & Galloway

The settlement, which is the seat of the Clan Douglas, was formerly called Carlingwark.

Cawdor   Highland

see Calder.

Cawdor Castle was the scene of King Duncan's murder in Shakespeare's *Macbeth*. Macbeth himself was Thane of Cawdor.

Ceres   Fife

obscure, but possibly 'black water'.
searach (Gaelic).

Chapel o' Garioch   Grampian

The name commemorates the former chapel dedicated to the Virgin Mary. Garioch is pronounced *geary*.

Clackmannan   Central

'stone of Manu'.

clach (Gaelic) stone.

Opinions differ on this, but it has been quite widely accepted that the *mannan* element refers to Manau, an area which was near the head of the Firth of Forth. There is a huge ancient stone in the town which bears the name Manu.

Cleish   Tayside

possibly 'a trench'.
clais (Gaelic) trench, furrow.

Coatbridge   Strathclyde

'bridge at a wood'.

coed (Brittonic) wood.

Lord Reith, first head of the BBC, was born here.

Cockenzie   Lothian

possibly 'Kenneth's corner'.

Coinnigh (Gaelic) Kenneth; *cuil* (Gaelic) corner.

This village's main claim to fame is its gigantic power station.

Cockpen   Lothian

'red head'.

coch (Brittonic) red; *ben* (Brittonic) head.

Coldstream   Borders

The name refers to the temperature of the River Tweed at this point. This village is right on the Scottish/English border. The Coldstream Guards started life here in 1659. Sir Alec Douglas Home, former Prime Minister of Great Britain, lives on his estate 'The Hirsel' close by.

Colonsay, Isle of   Strathclyde

probably 'St Columba's island', but possibly 'Kolbein's island'.

ey (Norse) island.

Comrie   Fife & Tayside

'confluence'.

comar (Gaelic) confluence.

Corrievreckan   Strathclyde

'corner land'.

cuil (Gaelic) corner; *tir* (Gaelic) land.

Cowdenbeath   Fife
'birch woods'.
coilltean (Gaelic) woods; *beithe* (Gaelic) birch.

Craigellachie   Grampian
'stony crag'.
creag (Gaelic) crag; *eiligh* (Gaelic) stony.

Crail   Fife
'rock'.
carr (Gaelic) rock; *all* (Gaelic) rock.

Crieff   Tayside
'branchy tree'.
craobh (Gaelic) branchy tree.

Culloden   Highland
'hollow of the pool'.
cwm (Brittonic) hollow; *lod* (Gaelic) pool.
Also called Drummossie. Here, Bonnie Prince Charlie's army was annihilated by the Duke of Cumberland's men in 1746, ending his bid to become king.

Culross   Fife
'holly wood'.
cuillenn (Gaelic) holly; *ros* (Brittonic) wood, point.

Cumbernauld   Strathclyde
'meeting of burns'.
comar (Gaelic) meeting, confluence; *allt* (Gaelic) burn, stream.

Cupar   Fife
'common pasture'.
comhpairt (Gaelic) common pasture; partnership.

Currie   Lothian
'boggy plain'.
currach (Gaelic) boggy plain.

D

Dalbeattie   Dumfries & Galloway

'field of the birchwood'.

dail (Gaelic) field, haugh; *beitheach* (Gaelic) of the birchwood.

Dalkeith   Lothian

'wood meadow'.

dol (Brittonic) field, meadow; *coed* (Brittonic) wood.

Dalmarnock   Strathclyde

'field of St Mernoc'.

dail (Gaelic) field, haugh.

Kilmarnock (Strathclyde) may also have the same derivation, but sources are unclear.

Dalry, St John's Town of   Dumfries & Galloway

'king's meadow', or maybe 'heather field'.

dail (Gaelic) field, haugh; *righ* (Gaelic) king; *fraoich* (Gaelic) heather.

The ancient St John's Stone in the main street has given its name to the town.

Deer Grampian

'forest'.

doire (Gaelic) forest.

The abbey here was founded in the Columban tradition and though it is far from clear if Columba ever visited the abbey, a local story says that the true meaning of 'Deer' is 'tear' (Gaelic – *deur*), which Columba is said to have shed as he left.

Dingwall Highland

'field of assembly'.

thing (Norse) parliament, assembly; *vollr* (Norse) field.

It seems likely that there was a Norse settlement here at one time.

Dollar Central

'ploughing field'.

dol (Brittonic) field, haugh; *ar* (Brittonic) ploughing.

The ruins of a castle with the irresistible name of Gloom stand here (usually called Castle Campbell nowadays).

Dornie Highland

'place of pebbles'.

dornach (Gaelic) pebbly; *dorn* (Gaelic) fist.

Dornoch Highland

has the same meaning as Dornie. A 'pebble' or 'handstone' is thought to have been just the right size to fit the fist.

The last official execution for witchcraft took place in Dornoch in 1722.

Douglas Strathclyde

'black stream'.

du (Brittonic) dark, black; *glas* (Brittonic) stream.

This is an appropriate name in a coal-mining area.

Drumelzier   Borders

possibly 'round hill'.

dun (Gaelic) hill, fortress, mound; *meall* (Gaelic) lump (of a small hill).

Formerly Dunmedler; Merlin, the wizard and seer, is supposed to be buried here. This one, however, may be a 6th-century Scottish twin to the 5th-century Welsh 'original'. Pronounced *drumellyer*.

Drummore   Dumfries & Galloway

'big ridge'.

druim (Gaelic) spine, ridge; *mor* (Gaelic) big.

Drumnadrochit   Highland

'bridge ridge'.

druim (Gaelic) spine, ridge; *drochaid* (Gaelic) bridge.

Dryburgh   Borders

'dry fort'.

drygge (Old English) dry; *burg* (Old English) fort.

The ruined, but still spectacular, abbey is the burial-place of Sir Walter Scott.

Dumbarton   Strathclyde

'hill or fortress of Britons'.

dun (Gaelic) hill, fortress, mound; *breatann* (Gaelic) of the Britons.

This is the ancient capital of the Britons in the kingdom of Strathclyde.

Dumfries   Dumfries & Galloway

'fort of the copse'.

dun (Gaelic) hill, fortress, mound; *phreas* (Gaelic) copse.

Some say that the *fries* element indicates a settlement by Frisians, but no conclusive proof exists. Robert Burns is buried here.

Dunbar   Lothian

'fort on the height'.

dun (Gaelic) hill, fortress, mound; *barr* (Gaelic) top, height.
The fort or castle is ancient and ruined.

Dunblane   Central

'hill of Blann'.

dun (Gaelic) hill, fortress, mound.
Blann lived in the sixth century. He was in charge of
the monastery at Dunblane.

Dundee   Tayside

'hill of Deagh'.

dun (Gaelic) hill, fortress, mound.

Dunfermline   Fife

possibly 'hill-land'.

dun (Gaelic) hill, fortress, mound; *lann* (Gaelic) land.
The *ferm* element may have something to do with tax
exacted on the land. Robert the Bruce is buried here.
Andrew Carnegie, the millionaire philanthropist, was
born here in 1835.

Dunkeld   Tayside

'fort of the Caledonians'.

dun (Gaelic) hill, fortress, mound; *Chailleann* (Gaelic) of the
Caledonians.

Dunoon   Strathclyde

'fort on the river'.

dun (Gaelic) hill, fortress, mound; *obhainn* (Gaelic) river,
water.
The river is the Clyde and the ruins of a very old castle
can be seen here.

Duns   Borders

'hill'.

dun (Gaelic) hill, fortress, mound.

The town lies at the bottom of a hill called Duns Law. The old town was on the hill itself, but was razed in 1545.

Dunsinane   Tayside

'hill of the breasts'.

dun (Gaelic) hill, fortress, mound; *sineachan* (Gaelic) breast.

Whither came Birnam Wood in Shakespeare's *Macbeth*.

Durness   Highland

'deer-cape'.

dyr (Norse) deer; *nes* (Norse) cape, headland.

This is almost as far north as you can go on the Scottish mainland and near the aptly-named Cape Wrath.

Dyce   Grampian

perhaps 'southwards'.

The Gaelic word is *deas*. The meaning may be 'cairn' (Norse – *dys*).

E

Earlston Borders

not 'Earl's town, but 'Ercil's hill'.

dun (Gaelic) hill, fortress, mound.

Formerly called Ercildoune. The ruins of Rhymer's Tower stand here. Thomas the Rhymer was a 13th-century poet.

Ecclefechan Dumfries & Galloway

'church of St Fiachan'.

eaglais (Gaelic) church.

Thomas Carlyle, the essayist and historian, was born here in 1795.

Ecclesmachan Lothian

'church of St Machan'.

eaglais (Gaelic) church.

Echt Grampian

possibly 'hilly place'.

eycht (Old English) hilly place.

The region is hilly and Barmekin of Echt, a hill with prehistoric fortifications, lies nearby.

Eddleston   Borders

'farm of Edulf'.

tun (Old English) farm.

The land was granted to Edulf, son of Utred, in the 12th century.

Edinburgh   Lothian

'fort on the slope'.

dun (Gaelic) hill, fortress, mound; *aodann* (Gaelic) slope.

The Gaelic form is Dun Eideann (cf. Dunedin in New Zealand). The castle was known as *Castellum puellarum* (castle of the maidens), so named, according to legend, because the daughters of chieftains were hidden there in time of war. There are such 'maiden' castles elsewhere.

Edinburgh is the capital city of Scotland.

Eigg, Isle of   Highland

'notched isle'.

eag (Gaelic) notch.

There is a 'notch' or depression running right across the island. Pronounced *egg*.

Elgin   Grampian

'little Ireland'.

Eilgin (Gaelic) little Ireland.

A part of Elgin was actually called little Ireland at one time.

Elie   Fife

'tomb'.

ealadh (Gaelic) tomb; *ayle* (Scots) covered cemetery.

There was once such a cemetery at Elie. Some graves were filled with precious items and from this sprang the Gaelic for treasure *ulaidh*. Pronounced *eely*.

Fettercairn   Grampian

'wood on a slope'.

fothair (Gaelic) slope, gradient; *carden* (Brittonic) wood, copse.

Macbeth's head was brought to King Malcolm at Fettercairn Castle.

Findhorn   Grampian

'white water'.

fionn (Gaelic) white; *eren* (Gaelic) water.

The *eren* element, often appearing as *earn*, is a common water name. The origin of the name is somewhat obscure. There may be a connection with Eire, or Ireland. Findhorn has twice been destroyed, once by encroaching sand and once by flood.

Fintry   Grampian & Central

'white homestead'.

fionn (Gaelic) white; *tref* (Brittonic) homestead, house, settlement.

Fochabers   Grampian

'boggy lake'.

fothach (Brittonic) lake; *abor* (Gaelic) bog, morass.

Forfar   Tayside

'watch-hill'.

fothair (Gaelic) slope, hill; *faire* (Gaelic) watching.

Forres   Grampian

'shrubbery', 'undergrowth'.

fo (Gaelic) under; *ras* (Gaelic) shrubbery.

Fort Augustus   Highland

Formerly Kilcummin ('church of St Cummein'), the town was renamed after Augustus, Duke of Cumberland, after the 1715 Rebellion. Fort Augustus stands on the road General Wade built to link Fort William with Inverness.

Fortingall   Tayside

'very strong church'.

fortrenn (Gaelic) very strong; *ceall* (Gaelic) cell, church.

The name of the Verturiones, a Pictish people, is preserved in Gaelic as *Fortrenn*. Legend has it that Pontius Pilate was born here.

Fortrose   Highland

'lower headland'.

foter (Gaelic) lower, under; *ros* (Gaelic) headland, cape, point.

Foyers   Highland

'slope'.

fothair (Gaelic) slope.

Fraserburgh   Grampian

Originally Faithlie, the name was changed when Sir Alexander Fraser bought the land in 1592.

Friockheim   Tayside

The story goes that the name comes from one Freke, who was a bailie in Forfar. It may be, however, simply a corruption of the Gaelic for heather *fraoch*. *Heim*, meaning 'home' in German, was added in 1830 by a John Andson, who had spent some time in Germany. Pronounced *freakam*.

Fyvie   Grampian

'path'.

fiamh (Gaelic) path, track.

33

G

Gairloch   Highland
'short loch'.
gearr (Gaelic) short.

Galashiels   Borders
'shielings by Gala Water'.
skali (Norse) hut, shieling.
The shielings were probably fishermen's homes.

Gareloch   Strathclyde
has the same meaning as Gairloch.

Gargunnock   Central
'little hill place'.
garradh (Gaelic) place, yard, enclosure; *dun* (Gaelic) hill,
fortress, mound; *-ock* is a diminutive suffix.

Garnock   Strathclyde
'little crying one'.
goir (Gaelic) cry; *-ock* is a diminutive suffix.

Garscadden   Strathclyde
'herring-yard'.
garradh (Gaelic) place, yard, enclosure; *sgadan* (Gaelic)
herring.

Gartsherrie   Strathclyde

'colt-field'.

garradh (Gaelic) place, yard, enclosure; *searraigh* (Gaelic) colt.

Garvald   Lothian

'rough, tumbling stream'.

allt (Gaelic) river, stream; *garbh* (Gaelic) rough.

Gatehouse of Fleet   Dumfries & Galloway

The town is on the Water of Fleet, which flows into Fleet Bay. 'Fleet' is probably from *fleot*, Old English for 'estuary'. Robert Burns wrote 'Scots wha ha'e' here.

Giffnock   Strathclyde

'little ridge'.

cefn (Brittonic) ridge; *-ock* is a diminutive suffix.

Gifford   Lothian

Though the village itself is only about 200 years old, the Gifford family had owned land in the area for centuries previously.

Gilchriston   Lothian

'Gilchrist's farm'.

gille-Criosd (Gaelic) servant of Christ; *tun* (Old English) farm, homestead.

Gilmerton   Lothian

'farm of Mary's servant'.

gille (Gaelic) servant, devotee; *Moire* (Gaelic) Mary – in this case, the Virgin Mary; *tun* (Old English) farm, homestead.

Girvan   Strathclyde
'rough river'.
garbh (Gaelic) rough; *allt* (Gaelic) river, stream.

Glamis   Tayside
'chasm'.
glamhus (Gaelic) wide gap, chasm.
Pronounced *glahmz*.
Glamis Castle is the seat of the Queen Mother's family.
Macbeth was Thane of Glamis.

Glasgow   Strathclyde
'green hollows'.
glas (Gaelic) green; *cau* (Gaelic) hollows.
This is the largest city in Scotland.

Glencoe   Highland
probably 'narrow glen'.
gleann (Gaelic) glen, valley; *comhann* (Gaelic) narrow.
The glen is also known popularly as 'the glen of weeping', in reference to the Glencoe Massacre in 1692, when a number of the Macdonalds of Glencoe were brutally murdered by Campbells. These two clans remain 'enemies'.

Gleneagles   Tayside
'glen of the church'.
gleann (Gaelic) glen, valley; *eaglais* (Gaelic) church.

Glenelg   Highland
'glen of Ireland'.
gleann (Gaelic) glen, valley; *elg* (Gaelic) Ireland.
Glenelg is the location of a very small car ferry, which crosses to Skye. The name is a palindrome.

Glenfinnan   Highland

'Fingon's glen'.

gleann (Gaelic) glen, valley.

Fingon was an abbot of Iona in the 14th century. Bonnie Prince Charlie raised the Royal Standard here in 1745, at the start of the '45 Rebellion. He was to fail in his bid to become king of Great Britain.

Glengarry   Highland

'rough water glen'.

gleann (Gaelic) glen, valley; *garbh* (Gaelic) rough (of water).

Glenlivet   Highland

'glen of the smooth place'.

gleann (Gaelic) glen, valley; *liobh* (Gaelic) smooth, slimy; *aite* (Gaelic) place.

This is the home of a very famous whisky distillery.

Glenrothes   Fife

'fort of the glen'.

gleann (Gaelic) glen, valley; *rath* (Gaelic) fort.

This is a new town with no glen.

Golspie   Highland

'Galli's farm'.

byr (Norse) farm, hamlet.

Gorebridge   Lothian

'bridge for goats'.

gobhar (Gaelic) goat.

Gourock   Strathclyde

maybe 'place of hillocks'.

guireoc (Gaelic) pimple.

Grangemouth   Central

'mouth of Grange Burn'.

The town is famed chiefly for its huge complex of oil installations and refineries.

Grantown-on-Spey   Highland

This model village on the River Spey was built in 1766 by the Grant family. Its former name was Freuchie – *fraochach* (Gaelic) place of heather. There is an existing Freuchie in Fife.

Greenock   Strathclyde

'sunny little place'.

grian (Gaelic) sunny land; *-ock* is a diminutive suffix.

James Watt, inventor of the steam engine, was born in Greenock in 1736.

Gretna Green   Dumfries & Galloway

'gravel hollow'.

greot (Old English) gravel; *holh* (Old English) hollow.

Gretna Green is famed as the border village where eloping couples came from England to be married quickly. Since the law was changed in 1856, a three-week waiting period has been necessary, thwarting many couples unaware of the new requirement, even in quite recent years.

Gruinard   Highland

'green firth'.

groenn (Norse) green; *fjordr* (Norse) firth, bay.

The tiny Gruinard Island in Gruinard Bay was infected with anthrax for military experimental purposes at the time of World War II. The island was only detoxified in 1987 and was declared 'free of contamination' in 1988. Pronounced *grooinard*.

Guardbridge   Fife
'yard bridge'.

Gullane   Lothian
'little lake'.
gollyn (Gaelic) lakelet.
There was once a small lake at Gullane.

H

Haddington   Lothian
'Hadding's farm'.
tun (Old English) farm, homestead.
John Knox is said to have been born here in 1505.

Haddo   Grampian
The name is a corruption of *half-davoch*. The *davoch*
or *dabhach* is a unit of land, reckoned by the number
of beasts that worked it.

Hamilton   Strathclyde
'Hamyll's farm'.
tun (Old English) farm, homestead.

Harris, Isles of Lewis   Western Isles
'high island'.
har (Norse) high.
The place has given its name to Harris tweed. It is the
southern part of Lewis-with-Harris.

Hatton   Grampian
'hall farm', where the laird or lord lived.
tun (Old English) farm, homestead.

Hawick   Borders
'hedge settlement'.
haga (Old English) hedge; *wic* (Old English) settlement, farm.

Helensburgh   Strathclyde
The settlement was named after Helen, wife of Sir James Colquhoun. John Logie Baird, the inventor of television, was born here in 1888.

Helmsdale   Highland
'Hjalmund's dale'.

Heriot   Lothian
probably 'gap'.
heregeat (Old English) gap.

Hobkirk   Borders
'church in a valley'.
hop (Norse) shelter, valley; *kirkja* (Norse) church.
Formerly known as Hopekirk.

Holyrood   Lothian
'holy cross'.
rod (Old English) cross.

Holywood   Dumfries & Galloway
'holy wood'.
An abbey was founded here in the 12th century by the Lord of Kirkconnel. The site was previously known as Dercongal (Congal's oak-copse). Congal was a follower of St Mungo.

Houston   Strathclyde

'Hugo's farm'.

tun (Old English) farm, homestead.

The Hugo referred to is Hugo de Paduinan.

Hoy, Isle of   Orkney

'high island'.

ha (Norse) high; *ey* (Norse) island.

Humbie   Lothian

probably 'Hundi's farm'.

byr (Norse) farm, hamlet.

Huntingtower   Tayside

The 15th-century castle of this name was formerly called Ruthven Castle, from where the Ruthven family hunted.

Huntly   Grampian

Originally a Berwickshire place-name, it was brought north by the Gordons of Huntly, after whom the dance 'The Gay Gordons' was named.

I

Ibrox   Strathclyde
'ford of the badger'.
ath (Gaelic) ford; *bruic* (Gaelic) of the badger.
This is the home of Glasgow Rangers Football Club.

Inch   Lothian & Grampian
'island'.
innis (Gaelic) island.

Inchcolm, Isle of   Fife
'Columba's isle'.
innis (Gaelic) island.
The now ruined abbey of St Columba was founded in
1123.

Inchmichael   Tayside
'Michael's pasture'.
innis (Gaelic) in this case, river meadow, pasture.

Inchnadamph   Highland
probably 'ox meadow'.
innis (Gaelic) in this case, river meadow, pasture; *damh*
(Gaelic) ox.

Ingliston   Lothian
'Ingialdr's farm'.
tun (Old English) farm, homestead.

Innerleithen   Borders
'mouth of the River Leithen'.
inbhir (Gaelic) river-mouth, confluence.
The river Leithen meets with the River Tweed here.

Insh   Highland
See Inch.

Insch   Grampian
See Inch.

Inveraray   Strathclyde
'mouth of the River Aray'.
inbhir (Gaelic) river-mouth, confluence.
Inveraray Castle is the seat of the Duke of Argyll. The town stands on Loch Fyne, a name dear to the heart of the kipper connoisseur.

Inverbeg   Strathclyde
'small river-mouth'.
inbhir (Gaelic) river-mouth, confluence; *beag* (Gaelic) small.

Inverbervie   Grampian
'mouth of the River Bervie'.
inbhir (Gaelic) river-mouth, confluence.

Invergarry   Highland

'rough river'.

inbhir (Gaelic) river-mouth, confluence; *garbh* (Gaelic) rough.

The now ruined Invergarry Castle belonged to the Macdonalds of Glengarry. Some of the family emigrated to Canada in the early 19th century and founded another Glengarry.

Invergordon   Highland

The settlement was named after Sir Alexander Gordon in the 18th century.

Inverkeithing   Fife

'mouth of the Keithing Burn'.

inbhir (Gaelic) river-mouth, confluence.

Inverness   Highland

'mouth of the River Ness'.

inbhir (Gaelic) river-mouth, confluence; *nesta* (Old Celtic) roaring one.

Inverurie   Grampian

'mouth of the River Urie'.

inbhir (Gaelic) river-mouth, confluence.

Iona, Isle of   Strathclyde

Columba chose this island to found a monastery in 563 and set about converting Scotland to Christianity. The origin of the name Iona is uncertain. It is thought to be a writer's error for Ioua. However, this may have been a convenient mistake, as Columba translated into Hebrew is Iona or Jonah, meaning a dove. In Gaelic the island is called *ey Colum cille* (island of the church of St Columba). It is the site of the oldest Christian burial ground in Scotland and of many kings' graves, including that of Duncan, supposedly murdered by Macbeth. It remains a place of pilgrimage.

Irongath   Central
'marsh-land'.
earann (Gaelic) land, portion; *gaoth* (Gaelic) bog, marsh.

Irongray   Dumfries & Galloway
maybe 'flock-land'.
earann (Gaelic) land, portion; *graidhe* (Gaelic) flock.

Irvine   Strathclyde
The town is called after the River Irvine, which may mean 'green water'.

Islay, Isle of   Strathclyde
'Ile's island'.
ey (Norse) island.

J

Jedburgh   Borders
'farm on the Jed'.
burh (Old English) enclosed area, farm.
The River Jed may derive its name from *gead*, Gaelic
for 'pike'.

John o' Groats   Highland
The name is supposedly a reference to John de Groot,
a Dutchman who lived here in the 16th century.

Jura, Isle of   Strathclyde
'Doirad's island'.
eileann (Gaelic) island;
or 'deer island'.
dyr (Norse) deer; *ey* (Norse) island.
The notorious Corryvreckan whirlpool lies off the
north coast.

K

Keith Grampian
'a wood'.
coed (Brittonic) wood.

Kelso Borders
'chalk hill'.
calchow (Old English) chalk hill.
A part of the town is still called the Chalkheugh.

Kemnay Grampian
'head of the plain'.
ceann (Gaelic) head, chief; *magh* (Gaelic) plain.

Kenmore Tayside
'big head'.
ceann (Gaelic) head, chief; *mor* (Gaelic) big.
Kenmore was formerly known as Balloch (Gaelic form *bealach*, meaning a pass).

Kennoway Fife
possibly 'main field'.
ceann (Gaelic) head, chief, main; *achadh* (Gaelic) field.

Kilbirnie   Strathclyde
'St Brendan's church'.
ceall (Gaelic) cell, church.

Kilbride, East and West   Strathclyde
'St Bride's church'.
ceall (Gaelic) cell, church.

Kilconquhar   Fife
'Conchobar's church'.
ceall (Gaelic) cell, church.
Pronounced *kinyuchar*.

Kilcreggan   Strathclyde
'church on the little rock'.
ceall (Gaelic) cell, church; *creagan* (Gaelic) little crag, rock.

Kildonan   several
'St Donan's church'.
ceall (Gaelic) cell, church.
St Donan was martyred in AD 617 on the Isle of Eigg. Gold was discovered in Kildonan, Sutherland, in 1868.

Kildrummy   Grampian
'end of the ridge'.
cionn (Gaelic) end; *druim* (Gaelic) ridge.
Formerly known as Kindrummie.

Killiecrankie   Tayside
'wood of aspens'.
coille (Gaelic) wood; *critheann* (Gaelic) aspen.

Killin Central
'white church'.

ceall (Gaelic) cell, church; *fionn* (Gaelic) white.

The meaning of this place name is much in doubt. As well as 'white church', it has also been suggested that it means 'church' or 'burial-place of St Fionn', although there is no record of such a person. The final possibility is 'church by the water' (*ceall linn*).

Kilmacolm Strathclyde
'church of my Columba'.

ceall (Gaelic) cell, church.

Kilmarnock Strathclyde
'church of my Ernon'.

ceall (Gaelic) cell, church.

Burns' first book of poems was published here. This is also the home of Johnnie Walker whisky.

Kilpatrick, Old Strathclyde
'old church of St Patrick'.

ceall (Gaelic) cell, church.

Legend has it that St Patrick was born here.

Kilwinning Strathclyde
'church of St Finnan'.

ceall (Gaelic) cell, church.

St Finnan was a sixth-century Irish saint.

Kincardine several
'at the head of the wood'.

cinn (Gaelic) at the head; *carden* (Brittonic) wood, copse.

Kincraig Highland
'at the head of the crag'.
cinn (Gaelic) at the head; *creag* (Gaelic) rock, crag.

King Edward Grampian
'at the head of the division'.
cinn (Gaelic) at the head; *eadaradh* (Gaelic) division.
Nothing to do with monarchs or potatoes, but a corruption of the Gaelic. From *cinn eadaradh*, it became Kinedart (the ruined castle of that name stands nearby) and finally, King Edward.

Kinghorn Fife
'at the head of the marsh'.
cinn (Gaelic) at the head; *gronn* (Gaelic) mud, marsh.
The name has been erroneously connected with King Alexander III, who died here after a fall in 1286.

Kinglassie Fife
'at the head of the stream'.
cinn (Gaelic) at the head; *glas* (Brittonic) water.
The town was once known as Goatmilk.

Kingussie Highland
'at the head of the fir-wood'.
cinn (Gaelic) at the head; *giubsach* (Gaelic) fir-wood.
Often mispronounced phonetically: *kinyoosy* is correct.

Kinloch Tayside
'at the head of the loch'.
cinn (Gaelic) at the head.

Kinloss   Grampian

'herbaceous headland'.

ceann (Gaelic) head; *lossa* (Gaelic) herbs.

Kinnoull   Tayside

'at the head of the crag'.

cinn (Gaelic) at the head; *alla* (Gaelic) crag.

Kinross   Tayside

'at the head of the cape'.

cinn (Gaelic) at the head; *ros* (Gaelic) cape, headland.

Mary, Queen of Scots, was imprisoned in the famous island castle of Loch Leven at Kinross.

Kintyre   Strathclyde

'at the head of the land'.

cinn (Gaelic) at the head; *tir* (Gaelic) land.

Familiar to many in the song 'Mull of Kintyre', composed by Paul McCartney.

Kippen   Central

'little block'.

ceap (Gaelic) stump, block.

Kirkcaldy   Fife

'castle on the hard hill'.

caer (Brittonic) fort, castle; *caled* (Brittonic) hard; *din* (Brittonic) hill, fort.

This was the birthplace, in 1723, of Adam Smith, author of *The Wealth of Nations*, and in 1728 of Robert Adam, master architect. Pronounced *kercoddy*.

Kirkcudbright   Dumfries & Galloway
'church of St Cuthbert'.
kirke (Old English) church.
St Cuthbert was a seventh-century English saint.
Pronounced *kercoobri*.

Kirkgunzeon   Dumfries & Galloway
'church of St Finnan'.
kirke (Old English) church.
This village lies on the banks of a stream called the
Kirkgunzeon Lane. Pronounced *kergunyan*.

Kirkintilloch   Strathclyde
'castle at the head of the hill'.
caer (Brittonic) castle, fort; *cinn* (Gaelic) at the head; *tulaich*
(Gaelic) of the hill.
The old name was Caerpentulach, incorporating 'pen'
(Brittonic, meaning 'at the head').

Kirkoswald   Strathclyde
'church of Oswald'.
kirke (Old English) church.
The   name   commemorates   King   Oswald   of
Northumbria, killed in battle in 642. This village has
many associations with Robert Burns. Two of his most
famous characters, 'Tam o' Shanter' and 'Souter
Johnnie' are buried here.

Kirriemuir   Tayside
'big quarter'.
ceathramh (Gaelic) a fourth (of land); *mor* (Gaelic) big.
This was the birthplace, in 1860, of Sir James Barrie,
author of *Peter Pan*.

Knockingallstane   Highland

'farm on the hill of the Comgalls'.

cnoc (Gaelic) hill; *tun* (Old English) farm, homestead.

The Comgalls may have been sixth-century settlers in Scotland.

Knoydart   Highland

'Cnut's fjord'.

-ord and *-art* were Gaelic forms of fjord.

Kyleakin   Highland

'straits of Hakon'.

caol (Gaelic) strait; slender.

Hakon was an early king of Norway, who sailed through the straits after his defeat at the battle of Largs in 1263.

Kyle of Lochalsh   Highland

'straits of Lochalsh'.

caol (Gaelic) strait; slender.

Lochalsh is still popularly believed to be derived from *aillse*, Gaelic for 'fairy'. This is unlikely and the true meaning remains obscure.

L

Ladykirk   Borders
'church of our Lady'.

The 15th-century church is said to have been built by James IV, in gratitude for his escape from death by drowning close by.

Laggan, Loch   Highland
'little hollow'.
lag (Gaelic) hollow.

Lairg   Highland
'shank'.
lorg (Gaelic) shank.

Lamancha   Borders

The name came into use through Admiral Cochrane, who had lived in the Spanish province of La Mancha in about 1736.

Lamlash   Isle of Arran, Strathclyde
'island of Molaisse'.
eileann (Gaelic) island.

Eileann has been reduced to 'lean'. *Molaisse* is a diminutive of *Laisren* with *mo* (my) attached. St Molaisse was abbot of Lethglend and died in 639.

Lanark   Strathclyde
'clearing'.
llanerch (Brittonic) clearing, glade.

Langholm   Dumfries & Galloway
'long meadow'.
holmr (Norse) meadow.
The poet Hugh MacDiarmid was born here.
Pronounced *langam*.

Larbert   Central
'half-wood'.
leth (Gaelic) half; *pert* (Brittonic) brake, thicket.

Largo, Upper and Lower   Fife
'field'.
learg (Gaelic) field, plain.
Alexander Selkirk, upon whose experiences Daniel
Defoe based his story of *Robinson Crusoe*, was born in
Lower Largo in 1676.

Lasswade   Lothian
'fold on a meadow'.
laes (Old English) ford, fold; *woed* (Old English) meadow.

Lauder   Borders
possibly 'elmwood at the water'.
leamh (Gaelic) elmwood; *dobhar* (Gaelic) water.
The town sits on the Leader Water.

Laurencekirk   Grampian
'church of St Laurentius'.
kirke (Old English) church.
St Laurentius was a third-century martyr.

Leadhills   Strathclyde

The area was once mined heavily for lead, as well as gold and silver.

Lerwick   Shetland

'mud bay'.

leir (Norse) mud; *vik* (Norse) bay.

Lerwick is the most northerly town in Britain and the scene every January of the ancient Norse festival of Up-Helly-A.

Leslie   Fife & Grampian

'garden of the pool'.

lios (Gaelic) garden; *linn* (Gaelic) pool.

Lesmahagow   Strathclyde

'church of St Fechin' or 'church of St Machute'.

eaglais (Gaelic) church.

Machute was also known as Mahago, but some authorities suggest that Fechin is reduced here to the affectionate form *Mo-Fhegu* (my Fechin).

Pronounced *Lezma**haygo***.

Letterfearn   Highland

'alder-hill'.

leitir (Gaelic) slope, hill-face; *fearna* (Gaelic) alder.

Leuchars   Fife

probably 'place of rushes'.

luachair (Gaelic) rushes.

Pronounced *loochers*.

Lewis, Isle of   Western Isles

'marshy ground'.

leog (Gaelic) marsh, surface water.

The island and the surrounding smaller islands are also known as 'The Lews'. The main island is joined to Harris.

Lincluden   Dumfries & Galloway

'pool on the Cluden'.

llyn (Brittonic) pool, lake.

Linlithgow   Lothian

'lake in a marshy field'.

llyn (Brittonic) lake, pool; *llyth* (Brittonic) soft, marshy; *cae* (Brittonic) enclosed field.

Mary, Queen of Scots, was born in Linlithgow Palace in 1542.

Linton, East and West   Lothian

maybe 'farm of the pool'.

llyn (Brittonic) pool, lake; *tun* (Old English) farm, homestead.

There may, however, be a connection with the Latin word *linum*, meaning flax.

Linwood   Strathclyde

'wood by the lake'.

llyn (Brittonic) pool, lake.

Lismore, Isle of   Strathclyde

'big garden'.

lios (Gaelic) garden; *mor* (Gaelic) big.

St Moluag, a contemporary of Columba, headed a community here. Lismore has been referred to as 'Paradise'.

Lochearnhead Central

'head of Loch Earn'.

This is a popular centre for water-skiing.

Lochinvar Dumfries & Galloway

'loch on the summit'.

barr (Gaelic) summit, height.

There are remains of an island castle here, associated with the famous ballad 'Young Lochinvar'.

Lochinver Highland

'place at the mouth of the loch'.

inbhir (Gaelic) river-mouth, confluence.

Lochnagar Grampian

'loch of the outcrop'.

gaire (Gaelic) outcrop.

Lochnagar is actually a mountain, named after one of its tiny lochs. The name may be familiar to some through Prince Charles' children's book *The Old Man of Lochnagar*.

Lockerbie Dumfries & Galloway

'Lockhart's farm'.

byr (Norse) farm, village

Lomond Strathclyde

'beacon'.

lumen (Brittonic) chimney, beacon.

Longniddry Lothian

'new church hamlet'.

lann (Brittonic) church, monastery; *nuadh* (Brittonic) new; *tref* (Brittonic) homestead, hamlet.

Lorne   Strathclyde

This was named after Loarn, one of the first Irish settlers in Scotland.

Lossiemouth   Grampian

'mouth of the River Lossie'.

luss (Gaelic) plant, herb.

Luce (Dumfries & Galloway) and Luss (Strathclyde) have the same meaning. Ramsay Macdonald, Prime Minister of Great Britain in 1924 and 1929-35, was born in Lossiemouth in 1866.

Luce, New   Dumfries & Galloway

See under Lossiemouth.

Lumphanan   Grampian

'St Finnan's land'.

lann (Gaelic) land, field.

There is a church dedicated to St Finnan here. Nearby is Macbeth's Cairn, where he was killed in 1057.

Luss   Strathclyde

See under Lossiemouth.

Lybster   Highland

'lee farm'.

ly (Norse) lee; *bolstadr* (Norse) farm, stead.

M

Macduff   Grampian
The town was previous known as Down, but in 1783 it
was renamed after James Duff, Earl of Fife.

Machrihanish   Strathclyde
'plain of the high headland'.
machair (Gaelic) plain; *har* (Norse) high; *nes* (Norse)
headland, cape;
or 'whispering plain'
sanas (Gaelic) whisper, secret.

Mallaig   Highland
maybe 'headland bay'
muli (Norse) mull, headland; *vik* (Norse) bay.

Markinch   Fife
'horse meadow'
marc (Gaelic) horse; *innis* (Gaelic) island, meadow.

Maryburgh   Highland
The settlement was named after Queen Mary in 1692.

Maryport   Dumfries & Galloway
There is a chapel here dedicated to the Virgin Mary.

Mauchline Strathclyde

'plain with a pool'.

magh (Gaelic) plain; *linn* (Gaelic) pool.

The town is very much associated with Robert Burns; it was once famous for its snuffboxes.

Maybole Strathclyde

'dangerous plain'.

magh (Gaelic) plain; *baoghail* (Gaelic) danger.

Mealfourvounie Highland

'hill of the cold heath'.

meall (Gaelic) moor, heath; *fuar* (Gaelic) cold; *mhonadh* (Gaelic) hill, lump.

Meigle Tayside

'boggy meadow'.

mign (Brittonic) bog, marsh; *dol* (Brittonic) meadow.

Local tradition has it that this is the burial-place of Queen Guinevere. Pronounced *meegle*.

Mearns Strathclyde

'moor'.

myrr (Norse) moor.

Melrose Borders

'bare promontory'.

maol (Gaelic) bare top, summit; *ros* (Gaelic) promontory, point.

It is said that Robert the Bruce's heart is interred under a window in the ruined abbey here.

Methil Fife

'boundary wood'.

maid (Brittonic) boundary; *coille* (Gaelic) wood.

Milngavie   Strathclyde

'windmill'.

muileann (Gaelic) mill; *goath* (Gaelic) wind.

Milngavie is considered one of the 'refined' areas of the Glasgow environs. Pronounced *milguy*.

Moffat   Dumfries & Galloway

'long plain'.

magh (Gaelic) plain; *fada* (Gaelic) long.

John Macadam, of tarmac fame, lived here.

Moidart   Highland

'muddy firth'.

moda (Norse) mud; *fjordr* (Norse) firth.

Moidart is famous mainly as the arrival place of Bonnie Prince Charlie in Scotland at the time of the ill-fated 1745 Rebellion.

Moncrieff   Tayside

'tree mountain'.

monadh (Gaelic) mountain, moor; *craobh* (Gaelic) tree.

Moniaive   Dumfries & Galloway

possibly 'quiet, mossy place'.

moine (Gaelic) mossy place, morass; *shamhach* (Gaelic) quiet, still.

This was the home of Annie Laurie, heroine of William Douglas, wife of the laird of Craigdarroch, and famed in song.

Monifieth   Tayside

'boggy moss'.

moine (Gaelic) mossy place, morass; *feith* (Gaelic) bog.

Montrose   Tayside

'moss on the promontory'.

moine (Gaelic) mossy place, morass; *ros* (Gaelic) promontory, headland.

Monymusk   Grampian

'muddy moss'.

moine (Gaelic) mossy place, morass; *musgach* (Gaelic) muddy.

This village has given its name to a Scottish country dance.

Monzie   Tayside

'corn-plain'.

magh (Gaelic) plain; *eadha* (Gaelic) corn.

Morar   Highland

'big water'.

mor (Gaelic) big; *dobhar* (Gaelic) water.

Morar is famous mainly for its beautiful white sands.

Morphie   Grampian

'place at the sea'.

morfa (Brittonic) place at the sea.

Moscow   Strathclyde

'hazel field'.

magh (Gaelic) plain, field; *coll* (Gaelic) hazel.

This village stands on a river that has been nicknamed 'the Volga' for so long that the name has passed into common usage.

Motherwell   Strathclyde
'Mother's well'.
Probably dedicated to the Virgin Mary, the site of the well is now marked by a plaque.

Moulin   Tayside
'bare summit'.
maol (Gaelic) bare top, summit.
Robert Louis Stevenson lived here for a while.

Mount Vernon   Strathclyde
This was named after the estate of George Washington in America.

Muck, Isle of   Highland
'island of pigs'.
muc (Gaelic) pig.

Muckle Flugga   Shetland
'big precipices'.
mykill (Norse) big; *flugga* (Norse) precipices.
The lighthouse here is the most northerly inhabited place in Britain.

Muir of Ord   Highland
'moor with the steep round hill'.
ord (Gaelic) steep, round hill.

Mull, Isle of   Strathclyde
probably 'bare summit'.
maol (Gaelic) bare top, summit.

Musselburgh   Lothian
'mussel town'.
burh (Old English) village, hamlet.

N

Nairn   Highland

The town stands on the River Nairn and was formerly
called Invernairn (mouth of the River Nairn). There
may be some connection with the Latin, *natare*, to
swim or float. The town has been said to mark a
division between the Highlands and the Lowlands.
Local tradition has it that one half of the town used to
speak Gaelic and the other half English.

Navity   Fife & Highland

'sacred place'.

This name is linked to the Gaulish word *nemeton*
(sacred place). A local story says that the final
judgment will take place on Navity Moor
(Highland).

Nevis   Highland

'water'.

This is an ancient Celtic word. There are various other
romantic interpretations of the name of this dramatic
area. The most popular seem to be 'venomous one',
'terrible' and also 'sky-touching peak'.
Ben Nevis is the highest mountain in Scotland.

New Abbey   Dumfries & Galloway

The Cistercian abbey here was built in the 13th
century and is also known as 'Sweetheart Abbey'.
Devorgilla, who founded the abbey, is buried here
with the heart of her husband – hence its romantic
alternative name.

Newbattle   Lothian

'new house'.

neowe (Old English) new; *botl* (Old English) house, building.

Newburgh   Grampian & Fife

'new village'.

neowe (Old English) new; *burh* (Old English) village, hamlet.

Newmachar   Grampian

St Machar was the saint of Aberdeen, where stands the cathedral of Old Machar. He was eventually made bishop of Tours.

Newtonmore   Highland

'new town on the moor'.

The name is simply an adaptation of English.

Niddrie   Lothian

'new settlement'.

nuadh (Brittonic) new; *tref* (Brittonic) settlement, village, hamlet.

Nigg   Grampian & Highland

'bay'.

vik (Norse) bay.

O

Oban   Strathclyde

'little bay'.

ob (Gaelic) bay; *an* is a diminutive suffix.

Ochiltree   Strathclyde

'high village'.

uchel (Brittonic) high; *tref* (Brittonic) village, settlement, hamlet.

George Douglas Brown, who wrote *The House with the Green Shutters*, was born here in 1869. John Knox was married here in 1564.

Ochtomore   Strathclyde

'the big eighth part'.

ochdamh (Gaelic) eighth part; *mor* (Gaelic) big.

Ogilvie   Tayside

'high plain'.

uchel (Brittonic) high; *fa* (Brittonic) plain.

Old Meldrum   Grampian

'old bare ridge'.

maol (Gaelic) bare; *druim* (Gaelic) ridge.

Orkney, Islands of

possibly 'island of the Orc or boar tribe'

ey (Norse) island;

or 'seal island'

orkn (Norse) seal.

The earliest form is *Orcas* (cf. the present adjectival form of 'Orcadian') in 320 BC. The Romans referred to the islands as the *Orcades*.

Oxnam   Borders

'ox meadow'.

holm (Old English) meadow.

Oxton   Borders

'Gilfalyn's farm'.

tun (Old English) farm, homestead.

The town was called Ulfkilston, which was rather spectacularly compressed to Oxton. Gilfalyn was Gillie Faolain, i.e. St Fillan's servant. St Cuthbert grew up here.

Oykell   Highland

'high'.

uchel (Brittonic) high.

Ptolemy, the second-century geographer, mentioned it as *Ripa Alta* (Latin for 'high banks').

P

Pabbay, Isle of   Western Isles
'island of the hermit'.
pap (Norse) hermit, priest; *ey* (Norse) island.

Paisley   Strathclyde
probably 'pasture plain'.
pasgell (Brittonic) pasture; *lledd* (Brittonic) plain;
or 'church'.
basilica (Latin) church.

Papa Stour, Isle of   Shetland
'great priest island'.
pap (Norse) hermit, priest; *ey* (Norse) island; *storr* (Norse)
great.

Patna   Strathclyde
This was named after Patna in India.

Peebles   Borders
'place of tents'.
pebyll (Brittonic) pavilion, tent.
This was the home of John Buchan, author of *The
Thirty-Nine Steps*, and of Robert Louis Stevenson.

Pencaitland   Lothian

possibly 'head of a clearing at a wood'.

pen (Brittonic) head, top; *coed* (Brittonic) grove, wood; *lann* (Brittonic) enclosure, clearing.

Penicuik   Lothian

'cuckoo-top'.

pen (Brittonic) head, top; *cog* (Brittonic) cuckoo.

The cotton industry in Scotland started here in 1778.

Pennan   Grampian

'hill-water'.

pen (Brittonic) head, top, hill; *-an* is often used as an ending to a water-name.

Large parts of the film *Local Hero* were made here.

Penpont   Dumfries & Galloway

'bridge-head'.

pen (Brittonic) head, top; *pons* (Latin) bridge.

Penpont lies on the path of an ancient pilgrimage route.

Perth   Tayside

'thicket'.

pert (Brittonic) brake, thicket.

Perth was formerly known as St Johnstoun – and the 15th-century church of St John still stands. Sir Walter Scott wrote of the town in *The Fair Maid of Perth*.

Peterhead   Grampian

'headland of St Peter'.

The ruins of the 12th-century St Peter's Kirk still stand here. The name has become associated in recent times with the prison.

Pettymuk   Grampian

'place of the pig'.

pett (Brittonic) place, part, share (of land); *muc* (Gaelic) pig.

Pett is a recognised Pictish Brittonic place name component. There are over 300 such names in the 'Pictish' areas of Scotland, mostly qualified by a Gaelic word, probably added by Gaelic-speaking settlers.

Pitcairn Green   Tayside

'land of the cairn'.

pett (Brittonic) place, part, share (of land).

A cairn is a pile of stones built in memory of the dead, or of some notable event, and also to mark boundaries. See Pettymuk.

Pitcaple   Grampian

'land of the mare'.

pett (Brittonic) place, part, share (of land); *capuill* (Gaelic) mare.

See Pettymuk.

Pitlochry   Tayside

'stony part'.

pett (Brittonic) place, part, share (of land); *cloichreach* (Gaelic) stony.

See Pettymuk.

Pittenweem   Fife

'cave land'.

pett (Brittonic) place, part, share (of land); *uamh* (Gaelic) cave.

St Fillan's cave-shrine is near Pittenweem harbour. The great architect Sir Robert Lorimer grew up here. See Pettymuk.

Plockton   Highland

'turf farm'.

ploc (Gaelic) clod, turf; *tun* (Old English) farm, homestead, hamlet.

Port Charlotte   Island of Islay, Strathclyde

The settlement was named after Lady Charlotte Campbell in 1828.

Portgordon   Grampian

The harbour was built by the Duke of Richmond and Gordon in 1874, and the place was named accordingly.

Portknockie   Grampian

'harbour by the little hill'.

cnoc (Gaelic) hill.

Portobello   Lothian

The name derives from Puerto Bello, a Panamanian town. A sailor who fought there under Admiral Vernon in 1739 gave his house the name, and this passed to the village in due course. Sir Harry Lauder was born here in 1870.

Portree   Isle of Skye, Highland

'harbour slope'.

ruighe (Gaelic) slope.

The name is often mistakenly thought to derive from *righ*, Gaelic for 'king', because of a visit from James V in 1540. This was also the scene of Bonnie Prince Charlie's farewell to Flora Macdonald in 1746. The town was formerly called Kiltaragleann (church of St Talarican in the glen).

Port Soy   Grampian

'warrior's port'.

saoi (Gaelic) warrior.

Marble quarried here was used in the building of the palace of Versailles.

Port William   Dumfries & Galloway

The settlement was founded by Sir William Maxwell in 1770.

Prestonpans   Lothian

'priest's farm'.

preost (Old English) priest; *tun* (Old English) farm, homestead, hamlet.

The suffix, *-pans*, refers to the salt-panning industry of the monks of Newbattle Abbey in the 12th century. Sir Walter Scott's *Waverley* describes the area.

Prestwick   Strathclyde

'priest place'.

preost (Old English) priest; *wic* (Old English) place, settlement.

Q

Quarrelton Strathclyde

'farm at the quarry'.

quareria (Latin) quarry; *tun* (Old English) farm, homestead, hamlet.

Queensferry, North and South Fife & Lothian

The queen referred to is the 11th-century Queen Margaret, King Malcolm Canmore's wife. Ferries no longer cross here, and the traffic goes by the Forth Road Bridge. Part of the action of Robert Louis Stevenson's *Kidnapped* takes place here.

Quinish Isle of Mull, Strathclyde

'sheep-fold headland'.

koi (Norse) sheep-fold; *nes* (Norse) headland, cape.

Quiraing Highland

'shieling by the sheep-fold'.

koi (Norse) sheep-fold; *airigh* (Gaelic) shieling.

R

Raasay   Isle of Skye, Highland
possibly 'roe-deer island'.
rar (Norse) roe-deer; *ey* (Norse) island.

Rannoch   Strathclyde, Highland & Tayside
'ferny place'.
raineach (Gaelic) fern.

Rattray   Tayside
'homestead at the fort'.
rath (Gaelic) fort, homestead, land; *tref* (Brittonic) homestead, hamlet, settlement.

Reay   Highland
'cattle/sheep-fold'.
rett (Norse) public fold.
Lord Reay, chief of Clan Mackay, took his name from here. The seat of the clan was Dounreay Castle, close by. Pronounced *ray*.

Renfrew   Strathclyde
'point of the stream'.
rhyn (Brittonic) point, cape; *frwd* (Brittonic) stream, torrent.
The Rivers Clyde and Gryfe flow together here. The Prince of Wales is Baron of Renfrew.

Romanno Bridge   Borders
'monk's homestead bridge'.
rath (Gaelic) homestead, land, fort; *manach* (Gaelic) monk.

Ronaldsay, North and South   Orkney
North Ronaldsay may be a corruption of Ninian, or
Ringan, and -*ey* (Norse for 'island'). South Ronaldsay
is said to refer to Ronald or Rognwald, who was
brother to a ninth-century Earl of Orkney.

Rosemarkie   Highland
'horse-headland'.
ros (Gaelic) cape, headland; *marc* (Gaelic) horse.

Roslin   Lothian
'morass at a pool'.
riasg (Gaelic) morass; *linn* (Gaelic) pool.
The village is also known as Rosslyn and is famous for
its chapel.

Rosyth   Fife
'cape of arrows'.
ros (Gaelic) cape, promontory; *saighead* (Gaelic) arrow.
There is a huge naval dockyard here.

Rothesay   Isle of Bute, Strathclyde
'Roderick's island'.
ey (Norse) island.
Roderick is Ruari or Rudri MacDonald. He was given
the island of Bute by King Hakon of Norway in the
13th century. Rothesay Castle was the original
'island', as it was surrounded by a moat. Prince
Charles is Duke of Rothesay.

Rothiemay   Grampian

'fort on the plain'.

rath (Gaelic) fort, homestead; *magh* (Gaelic) plain.

Rousay, Isle of   Orkney

'Rolf's island'.

ey (Norse) island.

Rowardennan   Central

'point of Adamnan's heights'.

rubha (Gaelic) point, cape; *ard* (Gaelic) height, hill.

The saint's name, Adamnan, has been shortened to *-ennan*. It is said that he stopped the spread of plague by plunging his crozier into the earth at a point in the village.

Roxburgh   Borders

'Hroc's castle'.

hroc (Old English) rook; *burh* (Old English) fortified village, hamlet.

The castle is now no more than a mound and there is no trace of the former village of Roxburgh. Hroc is a personal name, which also means 'the rook'.

Rum, Isle of   Highland

possibly 'projecting place'.

rhum (Brittonic) projection.

This meaning is by no means definite, but the island is certainly mountainous.

Rumbling Bridge   Tayside

The name comes from the sound of the River Devon here.

Rutherglen   Strathclyde

'red glen'.

ruadh (Gaelic) red.

Ruthwell   Dumfries & Galloway

'cross at a holy well'.

rod (Old English) cross.

The huge cross here is a 'preaching' cross, dating from the ninth century.

S

Saddell   Strathclyde

'priest's' or 'Somerled's meadow'.

sagart (Gaelic) priest; *dol* (Brittonic) meadow.

The small remains of a 12th-century Cistercian monastery are to be found here. The monastery is supposed to have been founded by Somerled, the first Lord of the Isles.

St Abb's   Borders

Aebba was the first abbess of Coldingham Priory close by (c.AD 650).

St Andrews   Fife

The town was first called Muckross (boar-wood), then Kilrymont (church on the royal mount), then Kilrule (church of St Regulus) and finally St Andrews after the church of St Andrew. It is now most famous as the 'home' of golf.

St Kilda, Isle of   Western Isles

There was no such saint. Apparently, the name arose from a well situated close to the mooring-place for boats. The well was called Tobar Childa: *tobar* (Gaelic) well; *kelda* (Norse) well. The original name of the island was Hort, which may mean 'death'. In view of the difficulties involved in reaching and living there, this is not an unlikely definition. The whole island was evacuated in 1930, but its dwellings are gradually being restored by volunteers. The island is also home to a missile tracking radar station.

St Monans   Fife

The town is probably named after Moinenn, the sixth-century bishop of Clonfert.

St Ninian's   Central

This is also known as St Ringan's (another form of Ninian). The famous battle of Bannockburn was fought close to here in 1314, when Robert the Bruce and his men defeated the army of Edward II.

Saltburn   Highland

The name recalls the days of salt tax, when, to evade payment of this, salt was smuggled ashore and hidden in burns.

Saltcoats   Strathclyde

'Coats' is a corruption of 'cottages' – these belonged to workers at the salt-pans. The saltworks were originally established here in the 16th century by James V.

Sanquhar   Dumfries & Galloway

'old fort'.
sean (Gaelic) old; *chaithar* (Gaelic) fort.

Scapa   Orkney

possibly 'shellfish bed'.
skel (Norse) shell (*scaup* (Scots) shellfish bed).

There were very productive oyster-beds here. Scapa Flow is best known as the naval base used during both World Wars.

Schiehallion   Tayside

'fairy hill of the Caledonians'.

sith (Gaelic) hill associated with fairies; *Chailleann* (Gaelic) Caledonians.

The *sidhe* (pronounced *shee*) or fairies are portrayed in a series of poems by W.B. Yeats, most chillingly in 'The Unappeasable Host'. But these are Irish fairies — the Scottish version seem to have been less alarming, for *sith* also means 'peace' in Gaelic.

Scone   Tayside

possibly 'lump'.

sgonn (Gaelic) mass, lump.

This may refer to the Mote Hill. The celebrated Stone of Scone, upon which Scottish kings were crowned, was taken to England in 1297, where it was placed under the Coronation Chair. It was returned to Scotland by nationalists in 1950, but was soon restored to Westminster Abbey, where it remains to this day. Some say, however, that the real stone is still in Scotland and the one at Westminster is bogus.

Scrabster   Highland

probably 'Skari's farm'.

bolstadr (Norse) farm, dwelling.

Selkirk   Borders

'hall church'.

sele (Old English) hall, court; *kirke* (Old English) church.

Shawbost   Isle of Lewis, Western Isles

'farm at the sea'.

sjar (Norse) the sea; *bolstadr* (Norse) farm, dwelling.

Shetland, Islands of

These hundred or so islands were known as Hjaltisland, from the personal name Hjalti. They are known also, though less commonly now, as Zetland. The *z* is the old Scots *y*, which, in turn, is the phonetic spelling of the Norse *hj*. Before the Norse invasion, they were known as *Inse Katt* (Cat Islands). The tribe of 'Cats' also occupied Caithness (*Katanes* i.e. Cat-cape).

Skelbo   Highland

'shell-farm'.
skel (Norse) shell; *bolstadr* (Norse) farm, dwelling.

Skirling   Borders

'rocky land'.
sker (Norse) rock; *lann* (Gaelic) land.
There is no connection with the sound of bagpipes.

Skye, Isle of   Highland

'winged island'.
sgiath (Gaelic) wing.
The name probably refers to the shape of the island. It is also known as 'The Misty Isle' for obvious reasons.

Slamannan   Central

'moor of Manu'.
sliabh (Gaelic) moor.
Manau is supposed to have been a district at the head of the Firth of Forth.

Sligachan   Isle of Skye, Highland

'place of shells'.
slige (Gaelic) shell.

Smailholm Borders
'small farm'.
smael (Old English) small; *ham* (Old English) village, farm.

Snizort Isle of Skye, Highland
'Sneis' place'.
The village was formerly called Sneisport. Sneis is a Norse personal name.

Society Lothian
The name is possibly a corruption of 'sea-city'.
The village lies on the shores of the Firth of Forth.

Sorbie Dumfries & Galloway
'mud farm'.
saur (Norse) mud, wet ground; *byr* (Norse) farm, village.

Sorn Strathclyde
'kiln'.
sorn (Gaelic) kiln.

Southend Strathclyde
Legend has it that this was where Columba first disembarked in Scotland. The meaning is obvious.

Staffa, Isle of Strathclyde
'island of staves'.
staf (Norse) stave, perpendicular column; *ey* (Norse) island.
This refers to the unusual basalt rock formations found here, one of which is Fingal's Cave, which inspired Mendelssohn to write his 'Hebrides Overture'. The name 'Fingal' is derived from Finn McCoul, the giant who is supposed to have constructed Staffa.

Stenhousemuir   Central
'stone house moor'.

Stirling   Central
possibly 'land by the stream'.
sruth (Gaelic) stream; *lann* (Gaelic) land, enclosure.
Stirling is known as 'The Gateway to the Highlands'.
Mary, Queen of Scots, was crowned here in 1543,
when she was nine months old.

Stonehaven   Grampian
'stony harbour'.
steinn (Norse) stone; *hofn* (Norse) harbour, haven.

Stornoway   Isle of Lewis, Western Isles
'steering bay'.
stjorn (Norse) steering; *vagr* (Norse) bay.
The name possibly refers to good marker points used
to guide a boat.

Stranraer   Dumfries & Galloway
'thick point'.
sron (Gaelic) point, nose; *reambar* (Gaelic) thick.
Sir John Ross, Arctic explorer (and ancestor of the
compiler of this book), lived here.

Strathaven   Strathclyde
'valley of the River Avon'.
srath (Gaelic) valley.
Pronounced *straven*.

Strathmiglo   Fife
'valley of the boggy loch'.
srath (Gaelic) valley; *mig* (Gaelic) bog; and *loch*.

Stromness   Orkney

'headland in the current'.

straumr (Norse) current; *nes* (Norse) point, headland.

Strontian   Highland

'point of the beacon'.

sron (Gaelic) point, nose; *teine* (Gaelic) beacon, fire.

The village gave its name to the mineral strontium, which was first discovered there in 1790.

Sullom Voe   Shetland

'bay of gannets'.

sule (Norse) gannet; *vagr* (Norse) bay.

Symington   several

'Simon's farm'.

tun (Old English) farm, homestead, hamlet.

T

Tain   Highland

This is an old Celtic name for water. The Tain Water runs close by the town. St Duthac's shrine at Tain was the focus for many royal pilgrimages, especially by James IV, in the 15th century.

Taransay, Isle of   Western Isles

'Taran's isle'.

ey (Norse) island.

The foundations of a small church called Teampull Tharain can be found here. It is said that the church was set aside for the use of women only.

Tarbert   several

'isthmus'.

tairbeart (Gaelic) isthmus, place of bringing over.

Tarbert (Strathclyde) was once the home of Robert the Bruce. Such, it is said, was the attraction of the isthmus as a crossing-place, that King Magnus of Norway had his boat dragged across (c.1093).

Taynuilt   Strathclyde

'house on the burn'.

tigh (Gaelic) house; *an uillt* (Gaelic) on the burn.

Pronounced *taynult*.

Temple   Lothian

This was the centre of the Knights Templar in Scotland in the 13th century. The order was abolished in 1312 and the land passed to the Knights of St John of Jerusalem.

Terregles   Dumfries & Galloway

'church hamlet'.

tref (Brittonic) homestead, hamlet, settlement; *yr eglwys* (Brittonic) with the church.

Thirlestane   Borders

'stone with a hole'.

thyrel (Old English) hole; *stan* (Old English) stone.

This may have meant a millstone.

Thundergay   Isle of Arran, Strathclyde

'windy hill'.

torr (Gaelic) hill; *na goith* (Gaelic) of the wind.

Thurso   Highland

probably 'bull river'.

thjorsa (Norse) bull river.

The town is situated on the River Thurso.

Tighnabruaich   Strathclyde

'house on the bank'.

tigh (Gaelic) house; *na bruaich* (Gaelic) on the bank.

Tillicoultry   Central

'back-land hillock'.

tulach (Gaelic) hillock; *cul* (Gaelic) back; *tir* (Gaelic) land.

Pronounced *tillicootri*.

Tingwall   Shetland

'field of assembly'.

thing (Norse) parliament, assembly; *vollr* (Norse) field.

Tinwald   Dumfries & Galloway

'meeting-place'.

See under Dingwall and Tingwall.

Tiree, Isle of   Strathclyde

'land of Eth'.

tir (Gaelic) land.

It is possible that the meaning may be 'land of corn', from the Gaelic *eadha*. This is an attractive definition in view of the island's former high productivity of grain crops.

Tobermory   Isle of Mull, Strathclyde

'Mary's well'.

tobar (Gaelic) well.

Tomatin   Highland

'juniper hillock'.

tom (Gaelic) hillock, knoll; *aitionn* (Gaelic) juniper.

Tomintoul   Grampian

'hillock like a barn'.

tom (Gaelic) hillock, knoll; *an t'sabhail* (Gaelic) like a barn.

This is the highest village in the Highlands, although not in Scotland. The roads around here are always amongst the first to be blocked by snow in winter.

Tongue   Highland

'spit of land'.

tunga (Norse) spit of land.

Tongue is also known as Kirkiboll (church farm).

Torphins   Grampian
'white hill'.

torr (Gaelic) hill, mound; *fionn* (Gaelic) white.

A local story claims that the name derives from Thorfinn, one of Macbeth's allies.

Tranent   Lothian
'homestead on the stream'.

tref (Brittonic) homestead, village; *nant* (Brittonic) stream, brook.

Traquair   Borders
'village on the River Quair'.

tref (Brittonic) homestead, village.

The 11th-century Traquair House (much extended over the following centuries) is the oldest inhabited house in Scotland. According to one of the picturesque stories attached to it, the gate to the main avenue was closed after the failure of the 1745 Rebellion, to remain so until a Stuart should be restored to the throne. It is closed to this day.

Troon   Strathclyde
'point'.

trwyn (Brittonic) point, nose.

The town does lie on a spit of land.

Tullibody   Central
'home on the hill'.

tulach (Gaelic) hill, hillock; *both* (Gaelic) homestead, bothy.

Tulloch   Highland
'hill'.

tulach (Gaelic) hill, hillock.

Turnberry Strathclyde

'tower at a town'.

turn (Norse) tower; *burh* (Old English) fortified town.

It is claimed that Robert the Bruce was born at Turnberry Castle. Turnberry is now most famous for its golf course, which hosts the British Open Golf Tournament from time to time.

Tyndrum Central

'house on the ridge'.

tigh (Gaelic) house; *an druim* (Gaelic) on the ridge.

U

Uddingston   Strathclyde
'Udd's farm'.
tun (Old English) farm, homestead, hamlet.

Uig   Isle of Skye, Highland, and Isle of Lewis,
Western Isles
'bay'.
uig (Gaelic) bay.

Ullapool   Highland
'Olaf's farm'.
bolstadr (Norse) farm, dwelling.
The village was founded in 1788 by the Fisheries
Association, to encourage the herring industry.

Urquhart   Grampian and Highland
'near a wood'.
ar (Brittonic) on, near; *carden* (Brittonic) wood, copse.
The English 'orchard' (Old English, *ortgeard*) stems
from this root.

V

Vatersay, Isle of   Western Isles
'glove isle'.
vottr (Norse) glove; *ey* (Norse) island.
Pronounced *fattersay*.

Voe   Shetland
'little bay'.
vagr (Norse) bay.

W

Wanlockhead   Dumfries & Galloway

'white slab'.

gwen (Brittonic) white; *lech* (Brittonic) slab, stone.

This is the highest village in Scotland. Gold and silver have been mined here.

Wemyss, East and West   Fife

'cave, hiding-place'.

uamh (Gaelic) cave.

There are many caves or *weems* on the coastline here. Near East Wemyss stands the ruin of Macduff's castle.

Westerkirk   Dumfries & Galloway

'west church'.

vestr (Norse) west; *kirkja* (Norse) church.

Thomas Telford, the famous engineer, was born here in 1757. Westerkirk is also known as Bentpath.

Westray, Isle of   Orkney

'west island'.

vestr (Norse) west; *ey* (Norse) island.

Whalsay, Isle of   Shetland

'whale island'.

hval (Norse) whale; *ey* (Norse) island.

Whitekirk   Lothian

'white church'.

kirke (Old English) church.

In 1914, suffragettes – amongst them the daughter of the minister – badly damaged the 15th-century church here. However, it was repaired beautifully by Lorimer, the master architect.

Whithorn   Dumfries & Galloway

'the White House'.

hwiterne (Old English) white house.

Formerly known as Candida Casa, the earliest Christian teaching in Scotland took place here from 397 under the guidance of Ninian. Whithorn was an important centre of religious teaching for a long time.

Wick   Highland

'bay'.

vik (Norse) bay.

Wigtown   Dumfries & Galloway

'farm homestead'.

wic (Old English) farm, settlement; *tun* (Old English) farm, homestead, hamlet.

Wormit   Fife

'the serpent'.

worm (Norse) serpent, snake; and *-et*, which is the article.

This is said to have been the first village in Scotland with electricity.

Wrath, Cape   Highland

'cape for turning'.

hverfa (Norse) to turn round.

The current pronunciation is very apt, in view of the severity of weather conditions around here.

Y

Yarrow   Borders
'rough river'.
garbh (Gaelic) rough (of a river).

Yell, Isle of   Shetland
'barren'.
geldr (Norse) barren.

Yetholm   Borders
'village at the gap'.
geat (Old English) gap, pass; *ham* (Old English) village, hamlet.
The village is divided into Kirk Yetholm and Town Yetholm. The former was once the seat of Scottish gypsies, where the 'Gypsy Queen', Esther Blythe, had her 'palace'. Pronounced *yettam*.

Yoker   Strathclyde
'lower ground'.
iochdar (Gaelic) lower part, ground.

Ythan Wells   Grampian
possibly 'gorse well'.
eith (Brittonic) gorse.
Pronounced *eyethan*.